THE HAND THAT HEALS THE BROKENHEARTED

A Story of Healing Through Christ After Loss

FELICIA GONZALEZ

Purelilly Press

This book is dedicated to
the loving memory of:

My son, Gabriel DeLaRosa II
05-08-1997 to 12-09-2023

and

My mother, Tammy R. Tewell
09-26-1961 to 05-12-2020

Contents

THE HAND THAT HEALS THE BROKENHEARTED

A short story of my journey from loss to healing by
Felicia Gonzalez, written in April 2024

He heals the brokenhearted and binds up their wounds.
Psalm 147:3 (NIV)

Prologue

Grief is not just about death; it encompasses all forms of loss. Many experiences in life can cause a person to grieve, and I believe everyone has encountered grief or knows someone who has. For instance, losing a cherished grandparent can be deeply painful, as grandparents often hold a special place in our hearts. Other examples of grief include the end of a significant relationship, losing a job, experiencing a serious illness, or moving away from a beloved home. Each of these losses can evoke profound feelings of grief and sorrow.

Let's not leave out pets; they can become like family. They are loyal and loving, and if you are like me, we always have a very special place for them in our hearts. I have two dogs and a cat, my fur babies. Their names are Buddy, Abby, and Lincoln. In addition, I have a goat named Billy. Billy is quite the character. If you met him, you would think he was terrific, too.

So many people have lost their places. I know some of us have lost homes due to floods, fires, or other acts of nature.

In today's economy, sometimes we deal with financial loss, which is why the loss of a job can cause grief, fear, and uncertainty.

Perhaps you have suffered the loss of your health from a horrible medical diagnosis. Losing your health can also cause grief. I have asthma and COPD. Unfortunately, Nicotine was not a good choice for me and has created a tough battle for me. I not only grieve the diagnosis but also the choices I made which caused the diagnosis. Perhaps you are also regretting past decisions and now grieving those choices.

Maybe you lost a relationship that was dear to you, such as in the case of a marriage where you ended up in a divorce, and you are now heartbroken and grieving the loss of that person in your life. Perhaps you decided to have an abortion that you deeply regret, or a child who died via miscarriage, or, like my son, a horrible accident. Many things in life cause heartbreak, grief, sadness, and a wide array of emotions, and we may need advice on how to get through them. That is precisely what my book is about: the story of what my heartache and grief came from, how I got through it, and an attempt to help you get through yours because none of us are alone in the hard times life can bring. Just remember, ***"My grace is sufficient for thee: for my strength is made perfect in weakness. Most gladly therefore will I rather glory in my infirmities, that the power of Christ may rest upon me."*** 2 Corinthians 12:9

This Book was inspired by the loss of my son in a tragic accident. Inside, you will find the story of his loss and my journey through grief, heartache, and the miracle Christ can do for us in the darkest times. We have all experienced some sort of loss in our lives, whether it be a loved one, a career, a marriage, or ourselves. I orchestrated this book to help you dive into your own story and journal your way through it. My book started out as a journal, but the Holy Spirit kept guiding my words, leading to what you are now holding in your hands - The Hand that Heals the Brokenhearted - because none of us have to be alone in times of sorrow. I truly hope my story will help you get through your sorrow and lead you to the healing that only Jesus Christ can provide.

With Love,

Felicia Gonzalez

That Gut Feeling

It was December 9, 2023. The entire day, I was carrying around this deep feeling in the pit of my stomach that something was very wrong. I'm sure we have all had this experience in our lives, knowing deep down that somewhere in the world, something is very wrong and the unrelenting anxiety of not knowing where, what, or who that gut feeling was concerning. My son Gabriel crossed my mind first. My son was dealing with some issues in life, as well as seizures. It made sense that he would be the first on my mind. As soon as this thought crossed my mind, he called. My mind felt some ease with that phone call. He was at McDonald's having some coffee before he got to things in his day. If I had known that would have been our last conversation, I would have kept him on the phone all day. He caught me early in the morning, and I was still lying in bed. "Mom, you sound tired. I'll call you back in a little while. I'm gonna finish my coffee and see if they have any work for me today," he said. I told him I was fine and would like to talk, but he was being his usual self and thinking of me. He told me to get my coffee and that he would call me later that day. We hung up.

I got up and went about my day thinking all was well, but I still couldn't shake that horrible feeling in my gut. What was it? Why won't it go away? My son is fine. My daughter was with me; my step-kids had checked in before bed the night before, and my husband and my sister were fine. Hours passed, and I texted my son to see what he was up to. I did not get a response. I thought to myself, "He probably found some work and is busy. I'll try back later." The day came to an end, and I still had not heard back from my son. I gave it the benefit of the doubt that he fell asleep after a long day of work. I finished my day and laid my head down. The deep gnawing in my stomach was still there. I prayed, "Lord, please take this feeling away and put your hand on whatever is going on that is causing it.".

5 a.m. on December 10th came around, and my husband's phone rang. He popped up to answer it, and it was my step-daughter. She had been in a car accident. She was right around the corner in our neighborhood, almost home. I thanked the Lord that she was okay and not seriously injured. This is why I was having that horrible feeling in my gut; something terrible just happened to one of our kids. She had hit a culvert at the edge of a driveway, rolled twice, and flipped her car up and over into a ditch. My husband went with her to the hospital. The police did a preliminary check and released her. She made it out with only a few scratches and bruises on her chest and legs from the airbags going off in the car. It was

over, and she was ok. So, why was this feeling still in the pit of my stomach? I decided to call my son and got no answer. "It is very early, so maybe he is still asleep," I tell myself aloud. The feeling in the pit of my stomach was starting to drive my anxiety through the roof. I kept reassuring myself that everything was okay and that it was all just because I was still shaken up over what had just happened to my stepdaughter, Ashley. "That's all it is. Right?" I thought.

Nevertheless, I called and texted my son all day. I sent him messages on Messenger through Facebook and text on his cell. I then called some of his friends and asked if they had heard from him. Still Nothing! Absolutely no response. His friends had not heard from him either. At this point, I was going into severe panic mode. Questions started to flood my mind, "Did he have a bad seizure? Is he okay? Is he in a hospital somewhere, and they don't have my information to call me? December 10th ended, and I still had not heard from my son. I could see that my son had not even read my messages. Something was very wrong.

That night, I barely slept. I kept opening my eyes at different times in the middle of the night to peek at my phone, hoping my son, Gabriel, had responded. My son sometimes suffered seizures, and sometimes, after a seizure, it would take him a day or two to recoup his mental state and become coherent again. I thought maybe this was the issue, but so much time had gone by, and still nothing!

It's now December 11th, the start of the third day. That feeling was still gnawing at me, and it was worse now. It felt like my stomach was being eaten from the inside, and I just wanted to pull my guts out to make this feeling go away. The morning light showed its face through my window; my husband was at work, and my daughter and stepdaughter were sleeping. I got up, made my morning coffee, and then went out to feed the animals. When I returned to the house, I pulled my phone out of my pocket to dial my son's number again. I saw that I had a missed call from an unknown number. When I saw I had missed the unknown number, I suddenly felt that it was not a seizure, and my heart sank into a bottomless pit of despair. I don't know how I knew mentally that it wasn't a hospital call, but I just knew. I knew I would get the worst news of my life.

As I write this, I realize that grief is not just about death; it is about loss. Many experiences in life can cause profound grief. Whether it's the loss of a loved one, the end of a significant relationship, losing a job, experiencing serious illness, or moving away from a cherished home, each loss brings its own form of sorrow.

Reflection

I invite you to take a moment to reflect on your own experiences of loss. Write about them, share them, and allow yourself to grieve. Healing begins when we acknowledge our pain and bring it to the surface to begin dealing with it. I know with God's help, you can do this.

Scripture

Philippians 4:6-7 (NIV)

"Do not be anxious about anything, but in every situation, by prayer and petition, with thanksgiving, present your requests to God. And the peace of God, which transcends all understanding, will guard your hearts and your minds in Christ Jesus."

Notes/Journal

What is your story? Think about what has caused you to go through fear and anxiety and make a thoughtful journal entry so you can begin to address this journey. We must go through it to come out of it.

____

____

____

____

____

____

2

The Call

The connections we have with our children are amazing. Parents have a special love for their children. This deep connection can act like an alarm system, giving us that gut feeling that something is not right, even if they are not in front of us to physically see them.

I believe wholeheartedly that God programs us with these amazing abilities, just like He is connected to all of us, HIS children, and He gave us the same gift with our children.

I prepared my fingers and strength to call the unknown number back. A lady answered the phone, and reluctantly, I asked, "I missed a call from this number?" deeply knowing it was bad. "And what is your name, ma'am?" the lady replied. I said, "My name is Felicia Gonzalez." She said, "Do you know Gabriel DeLaRosa? My name is Linda from the M.E.'s office."(She said this with little emotion.) The tears had already started streaming down my face. "Yes, I am his mother." And then the news that no parents ever want to receive, "Ma'am, we are sorry to inform you that Gabriel is deceased."

My knees buckled, and I hit the floor, crying in an uncontrollable fit. His sister came out of her room and saw me, and as if she already knew, she joined me on the floor with her tears streaming down her face. The lady at the Medical Examiner's office was still on the phone. I try to gather my voice and shattered mind together to ask what happened. She told me my son was killed on December 9th at around 8:30 p.m. as he was crossing the street. He was struck by a vehicle in a hit-and-run. That gut feeling! The who, what, and when was now established. It explained why he never replied. My ears were ringing. My face was hot with tears. I was shaking, and my heart had just been shattered beyond anything I had ever felt in my life. My boy, my firstborn, was only 26 years old and is now gone forever from this earth.

My daughter called my sister, and my stepdaughter called my husband. My husband came in from work immediately after receiving the call, and my sister, further away in Corpus Christi, came in a few days later. I was surrounded by my family, my daughter, husband, and stepchildren, but nothing made me feel better. In fact, it seemed as if I felt nothing at all, and time itself just stopped. I went completely numb. I refused to believe that this just happened to my son. I suppose, for many, that this is a normal reaction to such distressing, heart-wrenching news and the knowing that absolutely nothing could be done to change it. I know now I was in shock!

In Philippians 4, the Apostle Paul encourages the believers in Philippi to find joy and peace in the Lord despite their circumstances. The main lesson is to rely on God through prayer and thanksgiving and focus on life's positives and virtues. Paul emphasizes that God's peace will guard their hearts and minds in Christ Jesus and urges them to practice what they have learned and seen in him.

Reflection

The shock of finding out that I had lost my son and all the moments that went along with it, feeling as though my sorrow was uncontrollable and its depth never-ending, was extremely difficult. I know now that there is hope and healing through Jesus Christ. We can turn to God in prayer, and His peace, which surpasses all understanding, will be with us. This hope assures us that we are not alone, and that God's presence and peace are always available to us. God understands your pain and is with you in your suffering. He promises to be close to the brokenhearted and to save those who are crushed in spirit (Psalm 34:18). When the weight of your grief feels unbearable, turn to Him in prayer, just as Philippians 4:6-7 encourages. Pour out your heart to Him and allow His peace to envelop you. This peace may not erase the pain, but it can provide a comforting presence and a source of strength.

Scripture

Philippians 4:7 (NIV)

> *"And the peace of God, which transcends all understanding, will guard your hearts and your minds in Christ Jesus."*

Notes/Journal

How did you find out about your situation? What was your immediate reaction? How are you handling it today? Describe the moment you first learned of it, how it made you feel, and how you have processed or are still processing that grief. Let this be a step towards healing. Take this time to write down a prayer to God. Once you have finished, take a deep breath, and try to imagine what our loving God would answer and write it down. Sometimes, God talks in the small, still voice in the back of your mind.

____

____

____

____

3

Shock and Disbelief

Have you ever been in a situation where it felt like time just stood still, and existence itself seemed surreal? Shock does this. Well, at least it did to me. I went completely numb once the tears stopped. I found myself clinging to my daughter, my only child now, and to my husband, just trying to make sense of what had just happened to my son. I mentioned earlier the special connection God gives us with our children; this connection makes the loss even more profound.

As I think back, I reflect on my dreams about my son. For several years before his death, I remember having recurring dreams about Gabriel. In my dreams, I was looking at my son lying in a casket. My dream never told me what happened to him, only that he was gone. I always did my best to put those dreams aside, thinking they stemmed from anxiety. I had anxiety about his choices in life, and he struggled with seizures, depression, addiction, and mental illness. However,

I never thought that it would indeed come to pass. I know no one ever wants to believe that bad things will happen to them. We like to think ourselves exempt from the horrible things we see on the news or read about in news articles.

Anything can happen to anyone. Although we know bad things can happen to good people, it is hard to believe they can happen to us. Despite our best efforts to protect our children and ourselves, sometimes, it just doesn't work out the way we hoped. We try to accept that loss is a part of life, no matter how unfair it is.

Knowing these things happen every day makes me check on my kids daily to relay the messages of "Be careful," "Call me when you make it," "I love you," "What are you doing today?," "Make good choices." Knowing reminds me to pray for them, offer them advice, and so on, as if my words would shield them from harm in this world. Something in me believed that the things I saw on the news would never come into our home. I was not prepared for the pain that so many must endure in life when it actually showed up at my door.

Death is brutal for anyone to accept on its own, but when it comes suddenly to someone dear to you, it is compounded. And when it is your child, it is almost unbearable. We have all heard the phrase, "We are not supposed to bury our children." I can attest that it is a true statement, and I know that the loss of those whom we love dearly is extremely hard to accept, painful, and life-altering.

Another loss I experienced, and is very difficult, is the loss of a parent. I know this because I just lost my mother four years ago, as of May 2024. Her death was also sudden and very unexpected. She was only 58 years old. I remember that

I had just talked to her about two hours before my phone started ringing off the hook. My sister was calling. I pulled up to work and got myself situated to call her back. I dialed her phone, and she answered and exclaimed, "Hey, Mom is gone!". I replied, "What do you mean Mom is gone? Where did she go?" She said, "No, Mom is dead!" As with my son, shock set in. I did not believe her and became angry that she would even say that to me. I would not allow myself to believe it was true. I told her to pick me up from work and take me to her. I knew I was in no state to drive at that moment, and I was not going to believe the news that she was deceased until I saw my mother myself. I couldn't shake off the disbelief. I kept replaying it in my mind, unable to accept that my mother was gone, especially since I had just spoken with her, and she sounded fine. In fact, she had told me she was coming to stay with me for a few days for a visit.

The coroners waited for us, which I am grateful for because it was an hour's drive, so I could verify what felt like an absurd notion that my mom was deceased. Unfortunately, upon arrival at my mom's friend's house, where she died, the coroners were waiting, and I saw my mom's lifeless body on the gurney and her bag packed on the floor with the clothes she was bringing to stay with me. Mom passed three days after Mother's Day in 2020. As it turned out, she had undiagnosed cardiovascular disease. The medical examiner autopsied my mother and said every main artery was clogged, and her heart was four times its normal size. I still think about her every day. There are so many times a day that I need her and want to call her for advice or to vent. When my mother was still here, we talked on the phone at the very least 15 times a day about anything and everything. The silence when she was no longer there was deafening.

I remember that when I got the news about my son, the first person I wanted to call was my mother. It was extremely difficult to internalize the fact that I would not be able to talk to my mother in a crisis or for any reason ever again. It was hard to imagine ever dealing with a situation without my mom there to support me. She was an extraordinarily strong person. Although my daughter, stepdaughters, and in-laws are very supportive and loving, nothing can replace that special connection and comfort we have with our mothers.

For so many of us, nobody can replace our strong bond with our mothers. After my son's death, no matter what I was feeling and how much I wanted to fall apart, I knew I had to pull myself together quickly because I was not the only person who had just lost someone. "I am still a mother, and my daughter needs me," I reminded myself. We had both lost two people whom we loved deeply in less time than we cared for. We spent a few days crying together and trying to process what happened. We shared memories of Gabriel: his crazy laughter, his weird ways, his one-of-a-kind clothing style, and more.

My daughter was greatly affected; she was very close to her brother. My daughter and son had been attending college together the prior semester. She was studying criminal justice, and he was studying physics. She did not go back the following semester. I imagine it would not be easy for her to walk around the campus she just shared with her brother, seeing him in her mind's eye.

Few human experiences are as complicated as grief and

sudden loss. Sometimes, to heal, we must delve into raw emotions and profound reflections of a soul grappling with pain because of the unthinkable loss or the unimagined departure of loved ones. Through the lens of a grief journal, we embark on a journey of remembrance, healing, and resilience.

Notes/Journal

Take a moment to think about a time when you experienced a significant loss or shock. Write about that moment in detail. What were you feeling? How did your body react? Who were you with? What did you do to cope? Allow yourself to express those emotions fully. Acknowledging and documenting these experiences can be a powerful step towards healing. Also, give yourself grace for your reactions. It's expected to be in shock when something happens you did not want to happen or expect to happen. Life would be unbearable if we always expected the worst. We go through life hoping for the best. There is no training for this, but all things are bearable with God.

4

❦

Planning a Funeral

All the shock that had previously overtaken me had to be thrown out the window because it was time to plan a funeral. I had to put myself in neutral so others could help steer me in the right direction. I felt utterly lost. In place of shock came disbelief and deep heartache. I was overcome with the reality and the disbelief that I was planning my son's funeral. This new reality was now at the forefront. So many questions and thoughts were running through my mind. "How do I do this? Is this really happening? I'm not ready for this! Pull it together, Felicia! The Lord has got you, and you will get through this!"

It was time for the family to discuss the next steps. My husband, some of my sisters-in-law, and I would have to discuss the cost of it all and where Gabriel should be buried!

Shock re-enters. My thoughts race. "Nope! This is not happening! I am not ready!" As we began discussing plans,

I found myself becoming incredibly angry. Anger is an ugly emotion. I felt this deep anger rising up in me, so much so that I did not think I would be able to control it. Anger was consuming my very core.

Reflecting on this chapter of my life, I tried to paint a vivid picture of the rollercoaster of shock, disbelief, and anger experienced in the aftermath of losing a loved one. I realized how overwhelming emotions can take hold in times of profound loss. Shock, disbelief, anger—they can consume us if we don't find a way to process them. For me, writing has been a crucial outlet.

Reflection

I've found solace in expressing my feelings openly in my journal. Coping mechanisms like writing and seeking support from loved ones have become invaluable tools in my journey through grief. Through it all, I'm learning to lean into the support systems around me and find moments of strength amidst the pain. What support systems do you have around you to help you? Remember, it can be a friend, a family member, a priest, a counselor, or going to a local grief share group. At the very least, you can walk into a church, be with people, and listen to the word of God concerning you. If you are angry, it is ok to talk about it and write it down, but do not act in anger. Take a moment and make a list of places you might go for help in times of need.

Scripture

In the book of Ecclesiastes in the Bible, King Solomon speaks to the inevitability of seasons of grief and mourning.

Ecclesiastes 3:1-4

> *"There is a time for everything, and a season for every activity under the heavens: a time to be born and a time to die, a time to plant and a time to uproot, a time to kill and a time to heal, a time to tear down and a time to build, a time to weep and a time to laugh, a time to mourn and a time to dance."*

This scripture reminds us that grief is a natural part of the human experience, and there is a time for every emotion we encounter along the journey.

Notes/Journal

Take a moment to write down some places you could go or people you could talk to for support.

____

____

____

5

❦

Unexpected Anger

Anger is not a good look for anyone. It has a way of bringing out the worst in us and affects the people around us, people we care about. Because of our anger over our situation, we unintentionally hurt them or cause unnecessary tension. It has been my experience that when working out of anger, we tend to say things that hurt others and behave in a way that makes it very difficult for others to want to be around us. I was not expecting to be angry through all of this. I did not expect this emotion to come into play in this situation. I only expected sadness and heartache.

Everyone was trying to help me make plans and comfort me and my daughter. Deep down, I knew that we were all hurting, that I was really hurting, but in my head, I felt enraged. I was angry that I couldn't change the situation, and I was angry at the person who killed my son. I thought, "How careless can a person be while driving, hitting someone with

32

your car, and then leaving the person you just ran over on the road like a dog?" Anger! Yes! I was full of rage, and my anger was fueled by pain. It was a beast I had to get control of.

I had so many questions running through my mind, and nothing made sense. This was not fair! My son had so much life ahead of him, and this should never have happened. Gabriel had been crossing streets on his own since middle school, so how did this happen? Who did it? Why did they not stop? Would he have survived if they had just stopped to render him aid? What kind of monster just leaves someone like that? I had irrational thoughts like, "I will get them for what they have done!" Like I said, anger has an ugly head.

Our Lord God has many things to say about this emotion and the horrible things it will do to our spirit.

"Refrain from anger and turn from wrath; do not fret—it leads only to evil." - Psalm 37:8 (NIV)

"Get rid of all bitterness, rage and anger, brawling and slander, along with every form of malice." - Ephesians 4:31 (NIV)

"...because human anger does not produce the righteousness that God desires." - James 1:20 (NIV)

I knew I could not let this emotion consume me. Having dealt with anger in the past, I know all too well the dark hole that it will drag you down into. It festers inside your soul and causes bitterness and numbness, and all of the beauty and joy in the world become nonexistent. It is a doorway for the enemy to cause nothing but chaos inside of us. We may never understand why such terrible things happen, but through it all, I know God's plans are much bigger than mine or anyone else's.

As He says Himself,

"Be still, and know that I am God" - Psalm 46:10 (NIV), as well *as*

"Trust in the Lord with all your heart and lean not on your own understanding." - Proverbs 3:5 (NIV)

This is not always easy, especially for a parent who feels they need to constantly take the wheel in parenting, no matter how old their children get, and they may feel that their prayers are just not answered fast enough. That leads back to **BE STILL!** God sees a much bigger picture, and it can weigh heavy at times when we just don't understand the lack of prayer response in dire times. I guess I expected miracles from every prayer I sent up. I had sent up many prayers regarding my son's well-being. However, even if we do not get the answer we want, or when we are not immediately answered, He is listening, even when we can't see that. It's His will, not ours, that is to be done. The crazy thing I realized after this happened to my son, in time, of course, is that God answered all my prayers at once. It is our instinct and our job to protect our children, and I felt like a failure. Prayer is a wonderful way to help cope with anger and loss, but it does not happen overnight dealing with such pain. It is in the most difficult times that we should pray. In time, it really does help. Take time with God and know that He is listening. This is having faith, faith that even when we can't see Him, we know He is there.

Reflection

Anger: the emotion that rears its ugly head, most times uncontrollably. How do you deal with anger when it arises? Do you have any special prayers or techniques that help you calm this emotion?

Scripture

James 1:19-20 (NIV)

"Everyone should be quick to listen, slow to speak and slow to become angry, because human anger does not produce the righteousness that God desires.

Notes/Journal

Take the time to acknowledge your anger, but then tell God about it and ask him to help you let it go and replace it with peace.

____

____

____

____

____

6

✦

Keeping the Faith

F aith does not always come easy, especially in life's most trying times when we want just to throw in the towel and bury our heads in isolation. As I stated, God answered all my prayers at once. I had been praying for my son. He had dealt with homelessness, addiction, seizures, severe depression, and suicidal ideations. He was diagnosed with Mania, PTSD, and manic depression. I prayed for him constantly, "Lord, please let my son have shelter tonight, please don't let him give in to his temptations this day, Lord please send food his way today, Lord, help him know his worth and that he is loved," and so on. I tried for years to get him help. There are not many avenues for people dealing with his situation. In the few places I did find for him, he found an excuse to leave. Addiction and depression are formidable adversaries to overcome. He got depressed because of his addictions and was dealing with addiction because he was depressed. It was a vicious cycle.

Every time I let him stay with me, he would struggle. He had horrible manic episodes that led to psych hospital stays, or he would do something to upset the neighbors, and they would call the sheriff's department to come and deal with him. His addiction would cause him to have bad cravings. When he got these cravings, it was nearly impossible to get him to cooperate and do the right thing. My husband and I tried to keep him preoccupied on our small farm with animals, chores, fishing trips, and many other things, but all of this was to no avail. He would be overwhelmed with his inner struggles, and he would leave home again, chasing his addiction to calm his mind for the day.

Trying to keep faith when our hearts are heavy with daily worry proves difficult, but it is possible. All I have ever wanted for my children is for them to be healthy and happy. So, I would have to remind myself that, according to the Bible, in Philippians 4:13 (NKJV), ***"I can do all things through Christ who strengthens me."***

His suicidal ideations would only get him help for a day or two at a psych hospital. Homeless shelters were only one night and on a first-come, first-serve basis, or he had no place to sleep. All the men's homes I found in our area would not accept him because he was on seizure medication. Certain medications are not allowed in a men's home. In my son's case, it meant to be rehabilitated from drugs because seizure medication is a controlled drug. It made us both feel helpless. As a mother, I felt beyond defeated that I could not help him or find him any proper help. On top of that, he couldn't even get Medicaid for aftercare or a constant supply of necessary medication or food stamps for the food needed because he had no children to care for or a stable address. The system is not much help for people in his situation, and the rehabilitation centers that help with every need that comes with addiction, like the mental illness side and being able to actually take his medication for seizures, are incredibly expensive. I read all too often of other parents in similar situations as the one I was in with my son. It's a heartbreaking thing to watch our children go through and feel so helpless, knowing the possibility of losing our child is only around the corner. I only had God and my faith to rely on, literally, hope and prayer. Our children are only lent to us from our heavenly Father, and I am grateful for the day I found God, or I would not have made it through this. Jesus and faith are essential needs in life. We are lost without our Lord. As much as I miss my son, I am grateful for the time I had him in my life, and I pray daily for continuous strength and never to lose my faith. Life is not easy for Christians; we only gain the armor needed to deal with all the tribulations that come our way. We are soldiers for Christ, and a soldier's job is never easy. I figure Job, for example. He lost literally everything. The enemy thought he could turn Job against God, but our Father, having belief in Job and his dedication and faithfulness to the Lord in all situations, gave the enemy permission to test Job and pursue his agenda to turn Job against God. In the story, Job lost all his children, his home, and all his herds of animals. He even became extremely ill, and yet he persevered in his faith that God was good. The Lord our God rewarded him greatly for his faith; everything he lost was restored, and then some. We may not always reap our rewards while here on earth, but our treasures are stored in Heaven. Do not lose faith; do not lose hope; you are not alone, and you are loved dearly.

Reflection

What do you think you need to begin your journey of faith? Or how do you think you can build a stronger faith? Has anyone been of help to you in your process?

Scripture

Hebrews 11:1 (NIV)

> *"Now faith is confidence in what we hope for and assurance about what we do not see."*

2 Corinthians 5:7 (NIV)

> *"For we live by faith, not by sight."*

Hebrews 11:6 (NIV)

> *"And without faith it is impossible to please God, because anyone who comes to him must believe that he exists and that he rewards those who earnestly seek him."*

Notes/Journal

Reflect on a time when you felt your faith was challenged. What circumstances made it difficult for you to hold onto your faith? How did you manage to persevere, and what role did prayer and scripture play in your journey? Consider the people, experiences, or spiritual practices that helped you stay connected to God. Write about how you can continue strengthening your faith, even in the face of life's greatest trials. How can you support others who are struggling to keep their faith?

7

Why? - The Investigation

The investigation into the driver was brief. It took several days for a detective to be assigned to the case. My sister had already started her own investigation by looking into cameras in the area and asking the local people if they had seen what had happened. Several people in the area said that all they knew was that it was a dark-colored SUV and that they did not stop.

The detective called me with as much information as my sister had already gathered, not much of anything. Most of the surrounding cameras were not working; others were not facing toward the intersection in which my son was hit. The one camera that caught the incident was a very blurry visual considering it was dark out, drizzling rain, and the camera was facing the headlights, causing the license plate and driver to be invisible. All that the camera could see was that it was a large, dark-colored SUV and my son being struck.

The detective with HPD also said that nothing fell off the vehicle, which is rare. There was not a shred of evidence to help them find the vehicle or its driver. The detective talked to people in the area, such as the local homeless people who stay there, the cashier inside the gas station my son was walking back from, and surrounding people in the apartments my son was walking towards. Not a single witness could give any information other than a young man was hit while crossing the street. Everyone who saw it believed the vehicle sped up at the yellow light so they would not have to stop at the red.

In a world where everyone records everything, at an intersection in a busy Houston area close to an airport, with so many dashcams in cars, absolutely nothing was captured of the incident. I had to accept the fact that this person would most likely never be brought to justice.

Reflection

I must continue to swallow my anger and pray. I now needed strength I was not even sure I had to forgive whoever did this. I must accept that I will never understand why this turned out the way it did. I realized that no matter how much I wanted things to be different, all was now fully in God's hands. I am not a person without sin, and forgiveness is not always easy but necessary for the other person and the health of our own souls.

Scripture

Isaiah 30:18 (NIV)

"For the Lord is a God of justice. Blessed are all who wait for Him."

Matthew 6:14

"For if you forgive other people when they sin against you, your heavenly Father will also forgive you."

Notes and Journal

Reflect on a time when you faced a situation where justice seemed elusive. How did you cope with the uncertainty and lack of closure? Consider the emotions you experienced during this time and how you managed to find peace despite the circumstances. Think about any lessons you learned from this experience and how it has shaped your perspective on forgiveness, resilience, and the unpredictability of life. Write about the steps you took to navigate through the challenges and how you found strength in the midst of adversity. How did your faith or support from others help you during this difficult time?

____

____

____

8

Grief and Its Many Faces

Grief is grief, no matter what the loss. Grief truly does have many faces: shock, disbelief, anger, sadness, guilt, and depression. I am still grieving, which is what led me to write about my journey dealing with my son's death. Grief does not always have to be about death. We grieve many things in life. Your grief, like mine, may be about losing a loved one, or you could have lost a pet, a home, a marriage, a career, etc. Grief affects us all in various ways. We have already discussed shock, disbelief, and anger. Now, let us get into the sadness. Sadness is as heavy as all the other emotions, and they all have different effects on our lives and our decisions. Sadness enveloped me in my daily life as we went to the viewing, to the funeral, and as I put my son's urn into the ground next to my mother. This emotion can easily affect your health and take over your life. I barely cried at the viewing; I could only stare at my son's lifeless body, bringing back disbelief. This moment also brought to the forefront every dream I had of this moment. The same casket, the same face, my son, gone, only now, I know how he died.

My family was there praying hard for my son's soul. The priest arrived and blessed his body, giving him his last rites. My daughter was sitting in the pews with her head low, and I am sure her thoughts were reeling with memories. I was trying my best to stay strong and not show that I felt like I was dying inside. I do not know why I felt like I could not show such emotion; maybe it was the fleeting thought that if I did, I would be unable to pick myself back up. I could not succumb to this pain. I also did not want my son looking down on me, feeling so much pain, as if he would be mad at himself for dying and feeling guilty that he just never listened and couldn't get his life together. I know this sounds silly, but these thoughts did cross my mind. I wanted my son to know it was okay to let go and to allow himself to go to Jesus.

In my case, sadness affected every part of my being. I did not want to eat, and I was having nightmares. Although I was not there to see the incident, I kept seeing my son getting hit and lying on the road every time I closed my eyes. It made matters worse that someone took a picture of my son lying in the middle of the road after the incident with a sheet over him and posted it on Facebook. I was not sleeping well at all. Some days, I was spiraling down fast. When I finally slept, I felt no sense of wanting to or having a reason to get up in the morning.

Then, another feeling crept in...guilt. Guilt can eat you alive. I was dealing with a lot of guilt because I felt like if I had done anything differently at any point in life, would it have changed what happened? If I had been able to keep him on the phone longer that morning when he called me while having his coffee, would it have affected the timeline and changed what happened? If I had told him to come back home, no matter how things were going, he would have never even been at that intersection and still be alive. Literally, just any different action, would he still be here with me? These were the lies of the enemy, placing blame on me. The Bible offers wisdom and comfort for such times. In Isaiah 43:18-19, God reminds us not to dwell on the past but to be open to the new things He is doing in our lives. Holding onto past regrets or guilt can prevent us from seeing the new paths God is creating for us, paths that lead to healing and restoration. God promises to make a way in the wilderness and streams in the wasteland, bringing hope and renewal even in the midst of our deepest sorrow.

Similarly, in Philippians 3:13-14, the Apostle Paul encourages us to forget what lies behind and to strain toward what is ahead. This doesn't mean we erase the memory of our loved ones or our experiences, but rather, we release the hold that past regrets and guilt have over us. By doing so, we can focus on the future God has for us and the calling He has placed on our lives.

Depression is associated with guilt. They seem to go hand in hand because it was my guilt that brought on the depression. Depression is like a dark cloud that takes over within us. It runs deep within and is continuous. I found myself smiling reluctantly when I didn't want to so that people would think I was okay. I partook in daily life when all I wanted to do was stay in my room and isolate myself from the world. I lost a lot of drive to do anything worthwhile. I lectured myself daily about how this could not continue. I would tell myself that I still must live. I must live for my Lord, for my daughter, for my husband, for my sister, and for myself. I don't want anyone to feel this pain I feel if I were to be lost. So now, I deal with feeling selfish because I am struggling to care.

As you can see, grief really does have so many stages and faces. I have been praying a lot more, trying to bring myself back to who I once was. I found a great prayer called The Seven Sorrows of Mary. If any mother could understand the pain of losing a child, it is our Holy Mother. She is the epitome of strength in this area and many others. Our Mother watched her Son, our Savior, suffer for our sins. She watched Him carry His own cross to His crucifixion, to be nailed to that cross, and to slowly suffer on that cross as He hung there dying, and she could do absolutely nothing for the sake of us and His purpose. Even though she knew His purpose, her heart was in immense pain because He was her Son. I use this rosary to share and meditate on the pain with the one person who knows all too well how much it hurts. She received no consolation at the foot of the cross. Here is a rendition of the Seven Sorrows of Mary.

The Seven Sorrows of Mary stated in the form of a prayer*:

Prayer of the Seven Sorrows of Mary

In the name of the Father, and of the Son, and of the Holy Spirit. Amen.

The First Sorrow: The Prophecy of Simeon

Dear Mother Mary, we contemplate the sorrow you felt when Simeon prophesied that a sword would pierce your soul. As you held your infant son, you were given a glimpse of the suffering to come. Help us to trust in God's plan even when we face pain and uncertainty.

Hail Mary, full of grace, the Lord is with thee. Blessed art thou among women, and blessed is the fruit of thy womb, Jesus. Holy Mary, Mother of God, pray for us sinners, now and at the hour of our death. Amen.

The Second Sorrow: The Flight into Egypt

Blessed Mother, we reflect on the fear and hardship you endured during the flight into Egypt, escaping Herod's wrath. You fled in the night, protecting Jesus from danger. Teach us to seek refuge in God during our times of trial and to trust in His providence.

Hail Mary, full of grace, the Lord is with thee. Blessed art thou among women, and blessed is the fruit of thy womb, Jesus. Holy Mary, Mother of God, pray for us sinners, now and at the hour of our death. Amen.

The Third Sorrow: The Loss of the Child Jesus in the Temple

Loving Mother, we ponder the anguish you felt when you lost Jesus for three days and the joy and relief upon finding Him in the temple. Help us to seek Jesus always and never to stray from His presence.

Hail Mary, full of grace, the Lord is with thee. Blessed art thou among women, and blessed is the fruit of thy womb, Jesus. Holy Mary, Mother of God, pray for us sinners, now and at the hour of our death. Amen.

The Fourth Sorrow: Mary Meets Jesus on the Way to Calvary

Compassionate Mother, we share in your sorrow as you met Jesus carrying His cross on the way to Calvary. Your heart broke seeing His pain, yet you remained a source of strength for Him. Help us to support others in their suffering and to carry our own crosses with faith.

Hail Mary, full of grace, the Lord is with thee. Blessed art thou among women, and blessed is the fruit of thy womb, Jesus. Holy Mary, Mother of God, pray for us sinners, now and at the hour of our death. Amen.

The Fifth Sorrow: The Crucifixion and Death of Jesus

Grieving Mother, we stand with you at the foot of the cross, witnessing the crucifixion and death of your beloved Son. Your heart was pierced as He gave His life for us. Help us to embrace the sacrifice of Jesus and to live lives worthy of His love.

Hail Mary, full of grace, the Lord is with thee. Blessed art thou among women, and blessed is the fruit of thy womb,

Jesus. Holy Mary, Mother of God, pray for us sinners, now and at the hour of our death. Amen.

The Sixth Sorrow: The Body of Jesus Being Taken Down from the Cross

Tender Mother, we meditate on the sorrow you felt as you held the lifeless body of Jesus in your arms. The pain of loss was overwhelming, yet you accepted God's will. Help us to find comfort in God's embrace when we face the loss of loved ones.

Hail Mary, full of grace, the Lord is with thee. Blessed art thou among women, and blessed is the fruit of thy womb, Jesus. Holy Mary, Mother of God, pray for us sinners, now and at the hour of our death. Amen.

The Seventh Sorrow: The Burial of Jesus

Faithful Mother, we reflect on the sorrow of Jesus' burial, laying Him in the tomb and saying goodbye. Though filled with grief, you held onto hope in God's promise. Help us to remain hopeful in the resurrection and the life to come.

Hail Mary, full of grace, the Lord is with thee. Blessed art thou among women, and blessed is the fruit of thy womb, Jesus. Holy Mary, Mother of God, pray for us sinners, now and at the hour of our death. Amen.

Concluding Prayer:

O Sorrowful Mother, your heart was pierced by many sorrows. Through your suffering and faith, you teach us to endure our own trials with grace and trust in God. Intercede for us that we may receive the strength and peace of your Son, Jesus Christ. Amen.

In the name of the Father, and of the Son, and of the Holy Spirit.

Amen

Bibliography/Works Cited:

"Seven Sorrows of Mary." In The Catholic Encyclopedia. New York: Robert Appleton Company, 1912. Accessed [date]. http://www.newadvent.org/cathen/14151b.htm

I pray this prayer and know that our heavenly mother and our heavenly Father know my pain. I am thankful that at least I have my family to share my pain with, as we all share this pain together and each other's burdens.

Reflection

Grief is a multifaceted experience that touches every aspect of our lives. It is a journey marked by various emotions, from shock and disbelief to anger, sadness, guilt, and depression. Each emotion carries its weight and influence, shaping our responses and our healing processes. In my story, I tried to share the profound impact of losing a loved one, the heavy sadness that permeates daily life, and the consuming guilt that often accompanies such a loss.

In the face of such overwhelming sorrow, it is essential to remember that grief is a natural response to loss. It is a testament to our love and connection with the one person who is no longer with us. Sometimes, it is the loss of a relationship, job, or even a status. The journey through grief is deeply personal, yet it is also a shared experience. As you grapple with your emotions, you draw strength from your faith and the understanding that God is with you in your pain. The devotion to the Seven Sorrows of Mary provides a unique solace, as it allows you to connect with Mary, who understands the pain of losing a child. However, there are many places in the Bible where we can find stories like that of Job, who lost his status, his children, and his wealth. Jesus was ridiculed and mocked falsely.

Scripture

Isaiah 43:18-19 (NIV)

"Forget the former things; do not dwell on the past. See, I am doing a new thing! Now it springs up; do you not perceive it? I am making a way in the wilderness and streams in the wasteland."

This scripture reminds us that while it is natural to mourn and feel the weight of our grief, God calls us to look forward to the new things He is doing in our lives. He offers us hope and renewal, even in our most profound sorrow. By focusing on God's promises and His ability to bring about new paths and streams in the wasteland of our grief, we can find the strength to move forward.

Notes/Journal

Reflect on a time when you felt overwhelmed by grief and sorrow. How did you cope with those feelings? What steps did you take to begin healing? Write about how you have seen God work in your life during difficult times. Consider how the promise of new beginnings in Isaiah 43:18-19 can offer you hope and a way forward. How can you begin to let go of past regrets and embrace the new paths God is creating for you?

Use this journal entry to explore your emotions and find solace in the understanding that God is with you, making a way through your wilderness and providing streams of comfort and healing in your time of need. Remember, *"The Lord is close to the brokenhearted and saves those who are crushed in spirit."* - Psalm 34:18 (NIV)

9

Forgiveness

Forgiveness is not always easy, especially when we are trying to forgive someone who caused a life-altering wound. We must muster everything inside us to achieve this task and pray continually. Our Father is the only one who can provide such strength.

"Rejoice always, pray without ceasing, in everything give thanks; for this is the will of God in Christ Jesus for you."

1 Thessalonians 5:16-18 (NKJV)

Prayer really does build you up, even in the darkest of times. I have prayed continuously for my son's soul, for my ability to forgive, and for the forgiveness of the person who took him from me. I know the pain all too well of the loss of a child, and I am nobody to seek vengeance on another child of Our Most High God. I do not want my Father to lose that child when his or her judgment falls upon them, and I can only hope my prayer will open their heart to seeking true repentance for the actions that they took on that fateful day. This is one of our duties as Christians: to forgive fully, to forgive often, and to love as the Lord loves us, even to love our enemies.

Forgiveness is a process, however. It is not something that most of us achieve overnight while dealing with the pain of loss. Forgiveness means something different to everyone. For some, it can be true forgiveness toward whoever caused you the pain, and to some, it is just a decision to let go of your pain so you don't grow heavy inside and carry around bitterness. Either way, it fits for you; it is a critical step towards healing.

Holding grudges causes a bitterness inside that only grows. I came from a family where grudges were always held on the most minor things, and I did this as well because it was what I was taught. I went down a dark hole for years because of unforgiveness. It took a lot of work and a lot of years to get through the emotional rabbit hole and bring myself to where I am today. The people and lessons the Lord sent my way acted as vessels, giving me a guided tour and leading me to where I am now because we cannot overcome without our heavenly Father. I had to forgive the person who took my son that fateful night because He says we must forgive to be forgiven. I did not want ever to go back to that dark place within myself I had once been in. I had to remember that none of us are without sin, so none of us can cast stones. I chose not to let this dark incident take from me one more moment of peace in my life. I chose to give it to the Lord and to forgive.

Know that it is okay to grieve. It is understandable and expected to go through all these emotions, and maybe some other emotions that I did not mention when dealing with the loss of a child, any loved one, or any life-altering situation. It is okay to reach out when you just need someone to talk to. It is okay to have the need to forgive daily so it doesn't overwhelm your heart and soul. You should allow yourself to feel what you need to feel to come to a healthy conclusion in your grieving and forgiveness process. By the conclusion, I mean being able to finally cope and find joy in the memories instead of sadness and anger. As time goes by, it gets a little easier. We learn in time to cope with the pain and enjoy all the memories of our child or loved one. Remember, pray without ceasing. You are never alone in your heartache. Jesus is the ultimate comforter, and our Heavenly Father and Mary, our Mother, will always be there as well to share in your heartache and give you strength. Let them in. They want you to do so. As time goes on, you will find yourself moving towards peace with your pain.

Reflection

Forgiveness is one of the hardest commands we are given as Christians, especially when dealing with life-altering wounds. The journey to forgiveness is complex and demands strength, perseverance, and constant prayer. 1 Thessalonians 5:16-18 reminds us to *"Rejoice always, pray without ceasing, in every-thing give thanks; for this is the will of God in Christ Jesus for you."* (NKJV) Even in our darkest moments, prayer can guide us toward healing and forgiveness.

After losing my son, I turned to prayer for strength and for-giveness—not just for myself but also for the person respon-sible for my loss. The act of praying for them reflects Christ's command to love and forgive our enemies. Forgiveness is a gradual process requiring patience and God's support.

Holding onto grudges and resentment can fill our hearts with bitterness. My journey of overcoming a background of holding grudges shows how detrimental unforgiveness can be. Through God's grace, I found the strength to forgive and let go of bitterness. Forgiving the person who took my son's life brought healing and peace, reflecting trust in God's justice and a desire to remain in His peace.

Grieving is a natural part of healing. Emotions like sad-ness, anger, and guilt are valid and must be acknowledged. Seeking support and allowing yourself to experience these emotions is crucial. Forgiveness becomes a daily commitment that leads to the gradual release of pain and the embrace of peace. Over time, painful memories can transform into cherished recollections that bring joy.

Ultimately, the journey to forgiveness and healing is per-sonal and challenging. By maintaining constant prayer, I nav-igate this path with the assurance that I am never alone. Jesus, our comforter, alongside our Heavenly Father and Mary, our Mother, offers strength and solace. Allowing them into our hearts can lead us to peace, even in our pain.

Scripture

Ephesians 4:31-32 (NIV)

> *"Get rid of all bitterness, rage and anger, brawling and slander, along with every form of malice. Be kind and compassionate to one another, forgiving each other, just as in Christ God forgave you."*

Mark 11:25

> *"And when you stand praying, if you hold anything against anyone, forgive them, so that your Father in heaven may forgive you your sins."*

Ephesians 4:32 (NKJV)

> *"And be kind to one another, tenderhearted, forgiving one another, even as God in Christ forgave you"*

These scriptures encourage us to let go of negative emotions and embrace kindness, compassion, and forgiveness. It reminds us that forgiveness reflects God's forgiveness toward us, and by following this example, we can find peace and healing.

Notes/Journal

Reflect on your journey of forgiveness. What steps have you taken to forgive those who hurt you deeply? How has prayer played a role in this process? Write about the challenges you have faced and the ways in which you have felt God's presence and guidance. Consider the impact of holding onto bitterness versus the freedom that comes with forgiveness. How can you continue to cultivate a forgiving heart in your daily life? Use this journal entry to explore your emotions and thoughts, seeking God's wisdom and strength as you navigate this difficult but transformative journey. Ask yourself, who have you had to forgive in life? What did you do to be able to forgive? Have you truly forgiven whoever may have hurt you, or are you still working on this?

____

____

____

____

____

____

____

10

Helping Hands

We often find ourselves surrounded by family and friends during times of crisis. It can be very overwhelming when we just want to be alone in our thoughts, tears, and the flood of emotions coursing through our heads and hearts. We do our best to put on a bold attitude as if to show that we are okay, even when we just want them all to go away. However, as hard as it can be, and as overwhelming as it can feel, having such people around you is good. They are there to be our helping hands. As hard as it feels at the moment, let them in.

They are feeling just as much anxiety as you are because they are doing everything they can to try and help you feel better in a time where not a single word or action takes the pain away, yet they try anyway because they love you. You should also remember that they feel some of the pain and are trying to process how to help you. I have been around people who are hurting, all the while feeling like I was walking on eggshells. I felt that if I made the slightest error, whether with my tongue or with my movement, it would only make it worse. It was not an easy task. My family is a big advocate in striving not to let me or anyone else get lost in depression. As overwhelming as this can be at times, because it felt suffocating, it was and is a huge blessing. When we are lost in grief, we are usually our own worst enemies, and getting lost in painful thoughts only paves the way for that downward spiral that is very difficult to find our way back out of.

My family was truly a helping hand through the whole process, from keeping my mind occupied to helping plan the funeral process with phone calls, setting up appointments, and, most important of all, prayer. They all banded together, praying for my son's soul and my strength to get through the pain. As much as I wanted to be alone and drown myself in my pain, I am grateful they were all there to catch me. I would not have known how to make the funeral plans, how to get through seeing my son in his casket at his viewing, or the day I put my son's urn in the ground. They never ceased to remind me that I am strong, that the Lord has me in His arms, that I was not alone, and that I should trust in the Lord and have faith in His actions. They reminded me that even though my son is gone, it is not forever. It feels like forever before I will see him again in Heaven. However, our forever on earth lasts only as long as a snowflake on a hot day compared to the eternity that we will have together.

I know that not all of us have such strong families. My biological family was a complete disaster, to say the least, so when I married into the family I have today, I was blessed beyond compare. For those of you who do not have such people in your lives, know that you should reach out. There are many priests, grief counseling groups, support groups, and books you can read. For me, journaling and prayers have been a tremendous help. There are many avenues to finding help; you do not have to go through this alone. Remember, Christ says that you can do all things with Him, who will strengthen you. You are strong, so know that you can defeat the tug of wanting to give in to the pain and allow yourself to take the avenues needed to help you get through. You are so very important in our Father's eyes, and He is there for you, so don't give in to the enemy. Lean into those around you for help and support. Look for avenues that you can let your pain out that are constructive, like prayer and journaling. Do not make big decisions in this season without counsel. Remember, some decisions are irreversible.

Allowing all the helping hands you can find to guide you will lead you, in time, to be able to accept the situation and move you towards relishing in the beautiful memories of your lost loved one(s) and celebrating the time you had together. Moving on and accepting is a huge milestone during the course of loss and heartbreak. Remember, you got this, and if you are not familiar with special prayers for such occasions, just talk to Jesus. Just let it out! He wants you to talk to Him! You got this! You are strong! You are loved!

Reflection

In times of crisis and grief, it's natural to feel overwhelmed and want to retreat into solitude. But as difficult as it may be, allowing the support and love of family and friends can be a lifeline through the storm. Even when it feels suffocating or like walking on eggshells, their presence can provide comfort and strength. Remembering that they, too, are navigating their own anxieties and pain and trying to help can foster empathy and mutual support. Through prayer, shared burdens, and practical assistance, they become the helping hands that guide us through the darkest moments, reminding us of our resilience and the eternal hope we have in Christ.

Scripture

Acts 20:35 (NIV)

"In everything I did, I showed you that by this kind of hard work we must help the weak, remembering the words the Lord Jesus himself said: 'It is more blessed to give than to receive.'"

This verse reminds us to accept help, that we allow others to be blessed by allowing them to help us.

Philippians 4:13 (NIV)

"I can do all this through him who gives me strength."

This verse reassures us that in our weakest moments, we can draw upon the strength of Christ to endure and overcome. It reminds us that we are not alone in our struggles but rather empowered by God's presence and grace to face whatever challenges come our way. Through Him, we find the courage to lean on others for support and to navigate the journey of grief with faith and resilience.

Notes/Journal

Who are you grateful for in your life? Who has been a helping hand for you? What avenues have you used to get through your pain?

____

____

____

____

____

____

11

❧

Moving On and
Acceptance

When you begin to move on to acceptance, guilt may try to creep up because you may feel that remorse inside of leaving them behind. Know in your heart that you are not leaving your lost loved one behind; you are allowing them to move forward with the Lord as you continue to live the life the Lord still has in store for you. If it is a situation you are grieving, know that giving it to the Lord will allow you to move on in peace.

"Brothers and sisters, we do not want you to be uninformed about those who sleep in death, so that you do not grieve like the rest of mankind, who have no hope. For we believe that Jesus died and rose again, and so we believe that God will bring with Jesus those who have fallen asleep in him.

I Thessalonians 4:13-14

Everything our heart needs is in Jesus. It is truly okay to move on, forgive yourself, and leave the guilt. I like to think that our loved ones can look down on us from time to time, and if so, I know in my heart that my son and mother would not want to see me in pain daily but rather celebrate the life we had together while they were here. I know that throughout life, every time I have a memory of them or look at some old photos, there will be a piece of my heart that hurts because I want more than a picture or a memory, but this, I am sure, is normal. We miss them. We want to hug them. We want to tell them how much we love them and share news with them. The ultimate goal is not to let that pain consume us and to find peace in every situation.

Reflection

In our grief, it's natural to cling to memories and wish for more time with those we've lost. Yet, it's essential to balance this longing with the recognition that finding peace doesn't mean erasing the pain or memories but rather embracing them as part of our journey.

Finding peace amidst grief ultimately involves acknowledging that everything our heart needs is found in Jesus. It's about allowing ourselves to forgive, let go of guilt, and celebrate the lives we shared with our loved ones. While the pain of their absence may never fully fade, we can find solace in cherishing the memories and finding peace in every situation, knowing that they are always with us in spirit and that one day, we will be reunited in eternity.

Scripture

Psalm 34:18 (NIV)

> " *The Lord is close to the brokenhearted and saves those who are crushed in spirit.*"

Psalm 73:26 (NIV)

> "*My flesh and my heart may fail, but God is the strength of my heart and my portion forever.*"

Matthew 5:4

> "*Blessed are they that mourn: for they shall be comforted.*"

Matthew 11:28 (NIV)

> "*Come to me, all you who are weary and burdened, and I will give you rest.*"

Isaiah 40:31

> *"...but those who hope in the Lord will renew their strength. They will soar on wings like eagles; they will run and not grow weary, they will walk and not be faint."*

Just remember, you are never alone. You will get through this as I have. You are strong, you are loved, and we will see our loved ones again. Jesus loves you and is there for you! Mother Mary loves you and is there for you!

I love you all, and if we ever cross paths, I am here to pray with you and for you!

Notes/Journal

Think of comfort scriptures that have helped you get through. Open your bible, spend some time with God, and write what speaks to you on this healing journey.

____

____

____

____

____

I 2

Quotes

My son had a favorite quote that he would always remind me of when I was having a rough day. He came up with this quote in his own words, which made sense to his thought process. The original quote came from Kirk Scott, which is, "I can't change the direction of the wind, but I can adjust my sails to always reach my destination." His brain was an amazing machine with so much knowledge and imagination. His quote he came up with, I think, was to remind us that life can get stormy at times, but we can determine if we will sink or sail.

"The wind blows only when it wants to; it's up to you to learn to set your sails to catch it."

- Gabriel DeLaRosa

This is a good reminder that we can ride the storm with the right help. Jesus is always there for us. Our sails that catch the wind is prayer and faith. It's when we take our eyes off of Jesus that we sink. At least, this is how I look at his quote. It reminds me of the time Jesus put His hand out for Peter in the middle of the storm when Peter started to sink because he was more focused on the storm than his faith in Jesus. We can't let ourselves lose focus on what is important in life, or we will sink. When the storm comes, and it will because this is life, set your sails and ride the storm.

I also came up with a few quotes, which wasn't easy. Sometimes, things pop up in my head. I am not as creative as I'd like to be, but sometimes, trials in life need a positive outlook, and my brain comes up with stuff that makes sense. Two of my quotes have come from said storms:

"Sometimes chaos is necessary, as strength and character grow in the midst."

- Felicia Gonzalez

"Every man is a soldier. Nobody is left without at least one battle to face and fight."

- Felicia Gonzalez

There are many simple quotes in life that give quick insight into how to keep a positive outlook on life and its daily trials, however big or small they may be. Just a few that come to mind that stand out in a storm are:

"It's not what you look at that matters; it's what you see."

- Henry David Thoreau

"Difficult roads often lead to beautiful destinations."

- Zig Ziglar

"Life isn't about finding yourself. Life is about creating yourself."

- George Bernard Shaw

I look back and see that no matter how hard life was for my son, with all that he had dealt with, he was constantly creating himself. He was so smart. I know, as parents, we all say these things, but my son had a brain that I just could not comprehend. He was constantly learning by reading, studying, and asking questions. It was as if he could not learn enough. He taught himself several languages. He was not fluent but could have basic conversations in Spanish, Korean, and Japanese, and he was on his way to learning other languages. He understood physics and math on a level that allowed him to cover these topics with absolute ease. His dream was to be a physicist. He wanted to work for NASA one day. I have a nephew who is an intern in engineering at NASA and has some understanding of such things, and when I would hear them talk, it was like listening to a foreign language. I would have loved to see just how far my son would have made it in life, but that was not the plan that Our Father in Heaven had for him. Just like the quote from Allen Saunders says, "Life is what happens to us while we are making other plans." I have learned not to make plans in life. Nothing major. I am not saying I do not have goals, but I have learned in life that plans usually get messed up somehow. The small plans seem to have a way of not making it more often than not. It can get annoying, but as humans, maybe we miss the greater reason for these little blunders that come our way. I have also learned that life is more enjoyable when it is spontaneous. The spontaneity of daily life brings a sense of guessing and excitement, always wondering what is around the corner.

"It's good to be prepared, but spontaneity is very important – just to let yourself go and let it be whatever it is."

- Aron Eisenberg

However you choose to live your life, just remind your-self to live it fully, live it with love, live it with kindness and laughter, and stay grounded and humble. Love is the greatest gift you can give in a life that is never guaranteed another day.

Thank you for letting me share my journey of loss and grief with you.

Notes/Journal

Think of some quotes that have given you inspiration in life, a positive outlook, or just some strength. It is good to have more than one perspective on situations, goals, coping, etc. What are some of your favorite quotes, and in which ways did they inspire you?

____

____

____

____

____

____

____

13

Mindful Battles

I wanted to say something in reference to mental illness and even addiction, as for some of you, it might have hit a chord, or you may know someone who needs to hear this. A reference on trying to understand mental illness below is a picture that my son drew of how he said he felt constantly in his daily life, trying to get away from addiction and his own demons:

I know the feeling of being trapped in your own mind. I am sure many of you out there have had times like this in your own lives. I can see he was truly mentally trapped, and his drawing depicted the emotion and struggle very well. He was a very talented artist. The fact that I could not help him with this relentless battle was heartbreaking. He was on seizure medication, and this kept him from getting into the type of facility that would address his addiction. The constant seizures also made it difficult for him to work. Every time he got a job, he was so excited to be able to work, and then a seizure came while at work, and he was let go because he was considered a liability. I could see the defeat in his eyes every time. He also felt like he was fighting a losing battle. He had called me crying many times because of yet another job loss. I had been down the same road when I was young (not with seizures, but mental struggles). Although I was going through therapy at the time, took psych medication, and stayed in hospitals, none of it seemed to help. All it ever did was mask the issues for a temporary time and never brought forth a solution. Please do not misunderstand. I'm not downgrading therapy; having someone outside of the family to talk to is good because it takes the bias out of the conversation, and you can truly vent and get external advice. The true change came in my life, and the real answers came when I finally gave my life to God. I found solace and strength. I did everything I could to show my son, by example, what Jesus had done in my life. Ultimately, we must all make our own decisions on our life journey as adults. My son was finally on his path of seeking out scripture for comfort and strength, and I did see some change in him before he was taken from this world. I am thankful he was seeking assistance from our Father before his time ended here. We need Jesus in our lives. He truly is the ultimate healer and comforter. I reiterate the scripture, Matthew 11:28 (NIV), ***"Come to me, all you who are weary and burdened, and I will give you rest."*** And 2 Timothy 1:7 (NKJV)says, ***"For God has not given us a spirit of fear, but of power and of love and of a sound mind (self-control)"*** (emphasis added).

Food for Thought Before I Close My Story

If our Father in heaven has enough faith in us to withstand all the trials put in our paths, why not have the same faith in Him that He will carry us through? I crossed paths with a sweet elderly woman many years ago when I was going through my own struggles. As we got to talking, all the "Why me? Why me?" came out, and she asked me one simple question, "Why not you?" That was a critical thought for me, but that one conversation set me on my path to seeking the truth. I also had an employer who is very strong in faith who once told me, "Go to church every Sunday for three years. If nothing has changed in your life, then quit." I told myself I had nothing to lose, so I did, and I am a completely different, better person today. I still have moments of weakness, but my faith and my choices today in those weak moments are made with a stronger sense of discernment. It has now been over thirteen years, and I am not looking back. The Lord will send vessels your way, so keep your eyes and ears open so you don't miss the advice coming from the Holy Spirit. Remember:

YOU ARE STRONG!

YOU ARE LOVED!

YOU GOT THIS!

JESUS HAS GOT YOU!

14

Prayers

Here are a few prayers to help you out when your mind is just blank and overwhelmed.

Strength

All Powerful and ever-living God, the source of strength in our weakness, grant I persevere in the struggles of life and revive your Spirit burning within me, giving me all that I need. Enkindle within me this fire of Your love.

Amen

Healing

Loving and compassionate God, You reach your hand of healing to all those who are in need. Give me comfort in the times of my faith, and help me to feel the power of Your suffering and hope in the face of despair. Touch me with Your love now and always so that I may share it with all.

Amen

Bereavement Prayer

God do not let my feelings overwhelm me. During moments of anguish, touch my heart with courage, my soul with your compassion and with your love to comfort me. Despite my pain, let me know healing is occurring. Let me hear often that You are always with me. In Jesus' name,

Amen

O Lord, we call upon You in our time of sorrow that You give us the strength and will to bear our heavy burdens until we can again feel the warmth and love of Your divine compassion. Be mindful of us and have mercy on us while we struggle to comprehend life's hardships. In Jesus' name,

Amen

The Lord's Prayer

Our Father, who art in heaven, hallowed be Thy name. Thy kingdom come, Thy will be done, on earth as it is in heaven. Give us this day our daily bread, and forgive us our trespasses, as we forgive those that trespass against us, and lead us not into temptation, but deliver us from evil, for Thine is the kingdom, and the power, and the glory forever. In Jesus' name,

Amen

Journal to Your Heart's Content!

Has this book helped you in any way figure out a path to get through your grief journey? We cannot mask our grief; we must go through it and feel what comes so we can get through it and come out on the side of peace with our situation. It does get easier in time. Think of ways you have already begun to heal, and write down more ways you think you still need to heal. Everyone is different in their own beautiful way, and remember, it's okay to take all of the time you need to get through your heartache, grief, sorrow, loss, etc. Write whatever is on your mind; let it all out. Journaling is a great way to release so much within our minds and hearts that keeps us down. That is why this book started as a journal, and the Holy Spirit just kept putting more and more into my head, most likely to help anyone whose heart these words touched. Let the Lord lead the way!

____

____

____

Tribute

Rest in Beautiful
peace, My Son
Gabriel Delarosa, II
May 8, 1997 to
December 9, 2023

Sorry. Laughing
at myself

Rest in Beautiful
peace. My mom
Tammy R. Tewell
September 26, 1961 to
May 12, 2020

Epilogue

I was born and raised in Houston, TX. I have lived in Alvin for the last four years, and as a mom, I understand the roller-coaster. I am a housewife and live on a small farm that keeps me busy. I am on the way to being a second-time grandmother. I look for all the blessings the Lord sends my way. Seek yours out as well, and never let the darkness override the light that is our Lord. Thank you for letting me share my grief journey with you. For any mothers and fathers out there dealing with children in similar situations, know that I pray for you all, always, that the Lord lay His mighty hand on every situation and every person who needs comfort, strength, and guidance. Never give up! Know that God hears you, even when you think He doesn't. I love all of you, and may your life be full of faith, love, and laughter! If this small book can help even just one person, that will make this all worthwhile.